KU-253-902

CONTENTS

SHY GUIDES

THE SCIENCE OF QUIET PEOPLE

The Shy Guide to the Biology of Being Bashful

by Ruth Bjorklund

CHAPTER 1

UNDERSTANDING YOU

>>>>>>>

It's the first day of summer camp. Your parents have just dropped you off and said goodbye. You see other kids talking and laughing together. You would like to join in, but you feel very uncomfortable. You can't think of anything to say. You may even start to feel sick to your stomach. Your palms might feel sweaty.

Does this situation sound familiar to you? Have you experienced something like this? Maybe you just feel uncomfortable around people you don't know. Or maybe you just get nervous meeting new people or being in a crowd. You may even feel physically uncomfortable. But why?

First of all, you should understand that nothing is wrong with you. Lots of people are nervous in social situations. Everyone reacts differently to meeting new people. You may feel afraid. Many different systems are at work in your body when you feel afraid. Learning about them and being aware of your mind and body's responses can help you ease or overcome some of your feelings.

Raintree is an imprint of Capstone Global Library Limited, a company incorporated in England and Wales having its registered office at 264 Banbury Road, Oxford, OX2 7DY – Registered company number: 6695582

www.raintree.co.uk
myorders@raintree.co.uk

Edited by Abby Colich
Designed by Kay Fraser
Picture research by Morgan Walters
Production by Laura Manthe
Originated by Capstone Global Library
Printed and bound in India

ISBN 978 1 4747 6806 1
23 22 21 20 19
10 9 8 7 6 5 4 3 2 1

British Library Cataloguing in Publication Data
A full catalogue record for this book is available from the British Library.

Acknowledgements
We would like to thank the following for permission to reproduce photographs: iStockphoto: gawrav, 42, Koldunov, top 23, ModernNomads, 35, monkeybusinessimages, 6, RapidEye, top 17, skynesher, 21, SolStock, 13; Shutterstock: BlueRingMedia, 29, Christopher Edwin Nuzzaco, 9, 47, Daniel M Ernst, 3, 14, Dima Sidelnikov, 45, Everett Collection, 43, fizkes, 25, Ian Cramman, 11, Kathy Hutchins, bottom 23, Kosim Shukurov, 5, Leszek Glasner, 20, LINGTREN IMAGES, bottom 17, Lopolo, 19, Monkey Business Images, 41, Sanja Karin Music, 26, sciencepics, 34, Sebastian Kaulitzki, 27, 28, 38, Sky Antonio, 33, SpeedKingz, Cover, 1, whitehoune, 31, YakyCorbalan, 37

Every effort has been made to contact copyright holders of material reproduced in this book. Any omissions will be rectified in subsequent printings if notice is given to the publisher.

We would like to thank Christopher A. Flessner, PhD., Associate Professor, Department of Psychological Sciences and Director, Pediatric Anxiety Research Clinic (PARC) at Kent State University, Ohio, USA, for his help in the preparation of this book.

All the Internet addresses (URLs) given in this book were valid at the time of going to press. However, due to the dynamic nature of the Internet, some addresses may have changed, or sites may have changed or ceased to exist since publication. While the author and publisher regret any inconvenience this may cause readers, no responsibility for any such changes can be accepted by either the author or the publisher.

WHO YOU ARE

Have others described you as a quiet person? Before learning more about why your mind and body act the way they do, let's dive into what exactly it means to be a quiet person. You may have heard the terms shyness, introversion and social anxiety before. What's the difference between these? Which, if any, apply to you? Learning a little bit more about each of these may help you get to know yourself a little better.

>> Introvert or extrovert?

People may say you are shy or quiet. While that may be true, you may also be an introvert. Put simply, introverts get more energy being alone than they do from being around other people. Most introverts would agree that being alone reading in the library, going for a walk or adding music to their playlists is an ideal way to spend an afternoon. Introverts may be quiet around other people. They can also be outgoing. However, introverts usually have a limit to how much time they can spend around others. Too much time socializing can make them exhausted or even anxious. If you think you're an introvert, know that it's totally normal. Try to balance out your time socializing with being alone. Learn to recognize when you've spent too much time around others and need a break.

On the other hand, extroverts feel energized from being around other people. They like talking about their problems and are often more open about their feelings. Extroverts may be more comfortable in social situations and groups.

Some people are somewhere in between introverted and extroverted. They are ambiverted. They have qualities of both.

If you're not sure if you're an introvert, extrovert or ambivert, this quiz might help you find out.

True or False:

1. I prefer talking to people one-on-one.

2. I like being alone.

3. I am not good at small talk.

4. People tell me I'm a good listener.

5. I don't like a lot of changes or surprises.

6. I don't like having a party on my birthday.

7. I feel tired after being with friends even when I have had a good time.

8. I usually think about what to say before I say anything.

9. I do not like lessons that require class participation.

10. I do not like to make many plans for the weekends.

Count the number of true's you have. Then count the number of false's. If you have a lot more true's, you are more likely to be introverted. If you have an equal or nearly equal number, you may be an ambivert. If you have more false's, you are more likely to be extroverted.

However, it's important not to get too caught up in whether you're an introvert, extrovert or some of both. What's more important is to be comfortable with and confident in who you are. Focus on accepting yourself rather than trying to change into someone you're not.

SHYNESS

Shyness is different from being introverted. Both introverts and extroverts can be shy. Shyness is caused by fear and worry. Shy people may be afraid others will not like them. They may fear being judged or feeling embarrassed. Shy people may worry they will say stupid things. They often feel awkward and nervous around others, especially new people they haven't met before.

Some shy people may even have physical symptoms. Social situations may make them blush or sweat. Some people get an upset stomach or their heart may race.

As a result, shy people are more likely to avoid situations that make them uncomfortable, such as parties, class presentations or family gatherings. Others may see shy people as uninterested or rude. However, that's probably not the case. Shy people may actually want to be included and part of the conversation. They just need to find out how to overcome their fears.

Remember there is nothing wrong with being a bit shy. Nearly half of all people are at least a little shy. If you are shy or think you might be shy sometimes, find ways to ease into social situations. Find books to read about how to best handle social situations and meeting people. You can also ask a trusted adult for advice.

>>> Shy animals

Scientists have studied the behaviour of animals, including animals that seem shy. They have observed that shy animals watch and wait. Others go out into the unknown, without taking the time to observe their surroundings. In one experiment, biologist David Wilson dropped traps in a fishpond. Some fish were immediately curious and got caught. The shy fish were anxious about what was new and unfamiliar in their environment. They held back and were never captured. Some scientists believe this shows that shyness is actually important to the survival of some species.

>>>>> SOCIAL ANXIETY DISORDER

Everyone can feel anxious from time to time. Normal anxiety includes feelings of stress or worry about something. An upcoming test or a move to a new school are events that can cause anxiety. If you have anxiety that does not go away or lasts for long periods of time, then it may be considered a disorder. Anxiety disorders interfere with your everyday life. A person with an anxiety disorder may become too afraid or unable to do everyday activities. They may have trouble making friends or doing well in lessons that require participation.

Social anxiety disorder (SAD) is an extreme fear of social situations that does not go away. A person with SAD has extreme fear of and worry about everyday social situations, such as talking to people at school. People with SAD may also have extreme fears of being watched or judged by others. With the help of a therapist or medication, people with SAD can often overcome their fears and live happy, normal lives.

LIFE TIP

If you think you have social anxiety disorder or if you believe your anxiety is interfering with your daily life, ask a trusted adult for help. An adult can assist you in getting to a doctor or another professional who can help. You can also try the resources listed on page 46.

>>>> WHAT'S THE DIFFERENCE?

People who are shy, introverted or have social anxiety disorder may be labelled by others as quiet or bashful. However, it's important to understand the differences among these. Introversion and shyness are both personality traits. Introverts don't desire to be in social situations as much as extroverts do. Introverts may also be shy, but not all of them are. In fact, some extroverts are actually shy. Some shy people may have strong desires to be more sociable, but have fears that hold them back.

Shyness and social anxiety disorder are both rooted in fear. But social anxiety is an extreme fear. While shyness is a personality trait, doctors consider social anxiety disorder a mental health disorder.

While understanding these things is important, don't worry too much about whether you're introverted or not, shy or have some anxiety about social situations. (Unless you have a lot of anxiety that's interfering with your everyday life, then ask for help.) Focus more on accepting yourself. Think more about what your social goals are. Do you want to make more friends? Do you want to be involved in more social activities at school? Once you decide on your goals, you can work out ways to achieve them.

LIFE TIP

One way to help yourself break out of shyness is to join a group or club. Start with an activity that you are confident in and already know how to do. Then branch out by trying something new.

15

CHAPTER 2

>>>>>>>> **FIGHT OR FLIGHT?**

Think of a time you were in a social situation that made you feel uncomfortable. It may have been a classmate's birthday party or a group project for school. Did you feel frustrated because you wanted to leave, but couldn't? Did you feel nervous or self-conscious? Did your heart start beating faster? Could you feel your face turning red? Those uneasy feelings are the body's natural way of responding to fear and stress. Scientists call your body's responses to fear and stress "fight or flight".

Fight or flight was an important survival tool for prehistoric humans. Early humans gathered fruits and nuts and hunted wild game for food. If a hunter was faced with danger, such as a charging woolly mammoth, he or she acted on instinct. There was no time to think. Either the hunter had to attack the mammoth or run away from it. The human body's automatic fight or flight response gave the hunter extra energy and the strength to fight or flee.

Most humans today don't hunt for their own food. But other situations, such as social settings, still cause fear and anxiety. Your body's fight or flight responses are actually there to protect you when you feel this way. They are letting you know you need to make a decision to act.

>>>>> Prince Harry

Fight or flight responses can kick in for anyone, even a royal. Prince Harry grew up in the spotlight, but that didn't make him immune to the anxiety that comes with social situations for some people. He said in an interview, "In my case, every single time I was in any room with loads of people, which is quite often, I was just pouring with sweat, my heart beating – boom, boom, boom, boom – literally, just like a washing machine." After years of trying to hide his anxiety, Prince Harry finally got help from counselling. He is now an advocate for people dealing with mental health issues.

>>>>> FREEZING

Think back again to that social situation that made you uncomfortable. How did you respond? Did your flight response kick in and you left? Or maybe you tried to fight and took on the situation by saying whatever came to your mind? Or maybe neither of those things happened and you just froze.

Some experts have added "freeze" to the fight or flight response. Instead of tensing up and gathering the strength that the body needs to attack or flee, some people freeze instead. The response is similar to a deer stunned by the headlights of an oncoming car. For you, it may be standing in front of the class, speechless. Before the sweating and shaking starts, your body is trying to think about what it should do – fight or flee. Freezing was probably a fatal response for ancient hunters. However, as a modern-day human, it may give you a chance to collect your thoughts and calm down.

LIFE TIP

If you find yourself frozen in a social situation, first take a few deep breaths. Take a few moments to collect your thoughts and think about what to say. Make a list of lines you can use during these times. Try "I'm sorry, I lost my train of thought. Can you repeat that?" Or "Give me a second. I'm not sure what to say."

YOUR BODY'S RESPONSES TO FEAR

How someone physically reacts to fear can vary from person to person. Let's look at the various ways your body can respond and why.

Blushing: When frightened, certain body chemicals are released to increase strength. The chemicals cause more blood to flow. Because there are many blood vessels in the face and ears, the face and ears turn red.

Breathing rapidly: When fear strikes, the body switches from slow breaths drawn from the lower part of the lungs to faster, shorter breaths from the upper lungs. Rapid breathing pumps more oxygen into the muscles. But if someone is standing still and doesn't need extra oxygen, rapid breathing can cause light-headedness, confusion, and a "lump in the throat".

Stomach upset and diarrhoea: During times of fear and anxiety, the body releases extra amounts of a body chemical, called cortisol, which interferes with normal digestion. Your stomach produces extra acids to digest food quickly and give the body an energy boost.

Dry mouth: Fight or flight takes energy away from the parts of the body that are not needed for running or attacking, such as the stomach and the salivary glands, which make your spit. It gives any extra energy to the muscles. As well as making your mouth dry, this also explains why you may lack an appetite when you are stressed.

Headache: When threatened, the muscles of the body tighten, including the muscles across the forehead, causing a mild ache.

Rapid heartbeat: The heart beats rapidly to send more blood to the organs and muscles needed for action.

Muscle tension: As the body prepares for fight or flight, it takes blood away from parts of the body not needed for action and sends it to the large muscles. Parts of the body not needed for action include the shoulders, neck, jaw and face. Hunched shoulders, a stiff neck, clenched jaw and pursed lips are all because of reduced blood flow to these areas.

Shaky hands: When someone feels upset or afraid, the body sends out hormones. Hormones are chemicals that act like messengers. The hormones your body releases when it's afraid prepare some muscles for flight. But if you are not moving, your hormones are still racing around, making your muscles shake and tremble. This can make your hands shake.

Sweating: When the body uses a lot of energy, it gets overheated. Sweating cools the body. If you are standing in a room full of people, you are not running, but your body thinks you should be. Sweaty palms, forehead and armpits are the result.

Tingling and numbness: The fight or flight response pulls blood away from the skin and the extremities, including the face, hands and feet. Less blood causes tingling and numbness.

Voice quivering: Vocal cords in the throat are connected to a major nerve connected to a part of the brain that reacts to fear. The fight or flight response tightens the neck and throat and squeezes the vocal cords.

>>>>> Kevin Love

US basketball star Kevin Love has been open about his battle with the physical symptoms of his anxiety. He says one time his heart was racing so much he thought he was having a heart attack. He even lost consciousness. Love is working on treating his anxiety. He says talking with others about it openly and working with a therapist have helped him.

CHAPTER 3

THE BODY
IN ACTION

>>>>>>>>

Now you know the *what* and *why* of your body's response to fear. Your next question might be *how* does your body do it? Many different systems in your body are working together. The circulatory system keeps your blood moving. Your respiratory system keeps you breathing. These and several other body systems are busy when you feel fear or a threat. These body systems cause the many different physical symptoms in these situations. Learning about these body systems is an important part in understanding your body's response to fear in social situations.

>>>>> Just breathe

Your body's reaction to stress and threats is normal. But that doesn't mean you have to suffer every time your heart races or your palms get sweaty. You can work on changing your thoughts, which in turn can slow down or stop your body's responses. One way is to focus on your breathing. Taking slow, deep breaths can slow down your heart rate. Thinking calming or peaceful thoughts as you breathe may also help calm your mind.

THE CENTRAL NERVOUS SYSTEM

Your nervous system plays one of the most important roles in how your body responds to fear.

It controls the messages that go to your brain. The central nervous system is made up of the brain, the spinal cord and a network of nerves. Nerves are the pipelines that carry the body's messages to the brain and back to the body.

There are two main types of nerves – somatic and autonomic. Somatic nerves are ones you control, such as raising your hand in class. They also send messages to the brain, such as when you tell your brain you are scared that you're about to meet new people.

The autonomic nerves work differently. They send signals automatically. One autonomic nerve type carries most of your fight or flight messages. Do you get nervous meeting someone for the first time? Do you become unsure of what to say and get scared? It's these nerves that kick in. Another type of autonomic nerve helps calm you. When you start to feel better, these nerves send messages to return your breathing and blood flow to normal. Your heart rate will lower and your muscles will relax.

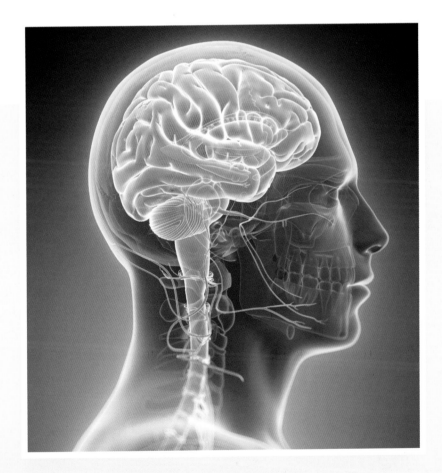

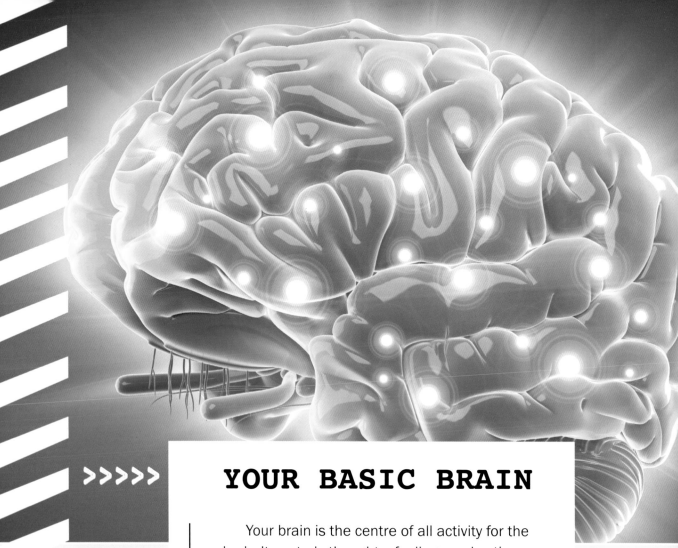

YOUR BASIC BRAIN

Your brain is the centre of all activity for the body. It controls thoughts, feelings and actions. To describe areas of the brain in the simplest way, scientists use a model called the "triune brain". The triune brain is divided into three basic parts.

The most basic part of the brain is called the reptile brain. The reptile brain does not think, it only acts. Its function is to control breathing, heartbeat, body temperature and balance. This part of the brain springs to action to prepare for a fight or flight response.

The middle brain, also called the limbic system, controls the chemicals that are in charge of emotions, memory and basic needs. When you feel threatened, the reptile brain tells the limbic system to release chemicals that will put the fight or flight response in motion.

The largest and most powerful part of the brain is the neocortex. It is a wrinkled grey mass that rests on top of the reptile and limbic parts of the brain. It is the centre for controlling thought, speech, language, creativity and other abilities. If you're in a social situation and you start to feel scared, your reptile brain takes over. It bypasses your neocortex. In the meantime, your neocortex analyses the situation. It decides there is no real threat to you. Then your body calms down.

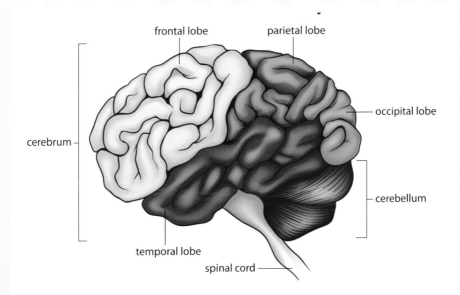

THE LIMBIC SYSTEM

The limbic system plays an essential role in your fight or flight responses. It has four main sections – the hippocampus, amygdala, hypothalamus and thalamus. The hippocampus is responsible for emotions and memories. The amygdala is like an alarm clock. It responds automatically to fear. It tells the hippocampus to remember threats and send those memories to the neocortex for storage. The hypothalamus sends the chemical messages that get your body moving. But when you feel threatened, those messages will tell your body to prepare to attack or run. The thalamus directs the flow of signals between the spinal cord and the brain.

Imagine walking through a shopping centre. You see a group of people from school. You really would like to join them, but you feel too shy to go and say hello. Even though they never see you and you never get near them, your limbic system remembers how you feel around them. It starts sending those dreaded fight or flight messages. And before you know it, you are sitting alone with sweaty palms and a rapidly beating heart.

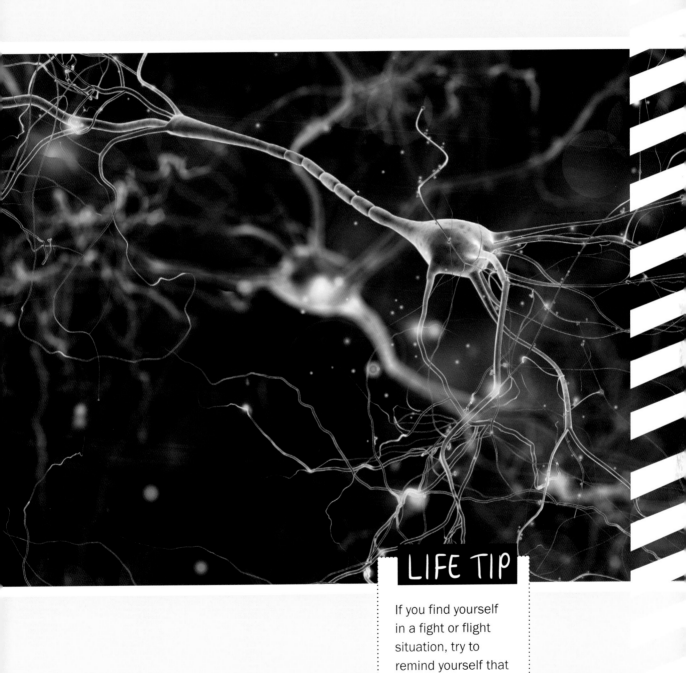

LIFE TIP

If you find yourself in a fight or flight situation, try to remind yourself that it will not last forever. This may help you calm down.

THE ENDOCRINE SYSTEM

Your endocrine system is made up of glands. Glands are small organs that produce substances such as sweat, tears and hormones. Hormones oversee growth, blood pressure, digestion, mood and more. When a person senses a threat, the limbic system sends fight or flight signals to the endocrine system. It tells your glands to launch hormones. The most powerful hormones in the fight or flight response are adrenaline, noradrenaline and cortisol. They are made in the adrenal glands and released into the bloodstream.

- *Adrenaline* gives you a surge of energy. Your muscles get tense. Your breathing gets faster. Your heart rate goes up. You begin to sweat.

- *Noradrenaline* makes you more sensitive and aware. It also directs blood away from the skin, muscles and organs not needed to fight or flee.

- *Cortisol* is called the "stress hormone". It shuts down digestion and raises blood pressure. Another hormone, made in the thyroid gland, gives the order to release extra fats and sugar into the blood for more energy.

>>> Adrenaline rush

Have you ever seen someone in a film pick up a car and lift it over his head? In real life, there have been some cases of people lifting up a car to free someone trapped underneath. This is sometimes called "hysterical strength". It is the rapid release of adrenaline, also called an "adrenaline rush", that gives a person this momentary strength. It is also the same "adrenaline rush" someone feels when engaging in daring or risky behaviour. Those who go skydiving or bungee jumping might talk about experiencing a surge of excitement or fear, which is their adrenaline kicking in.

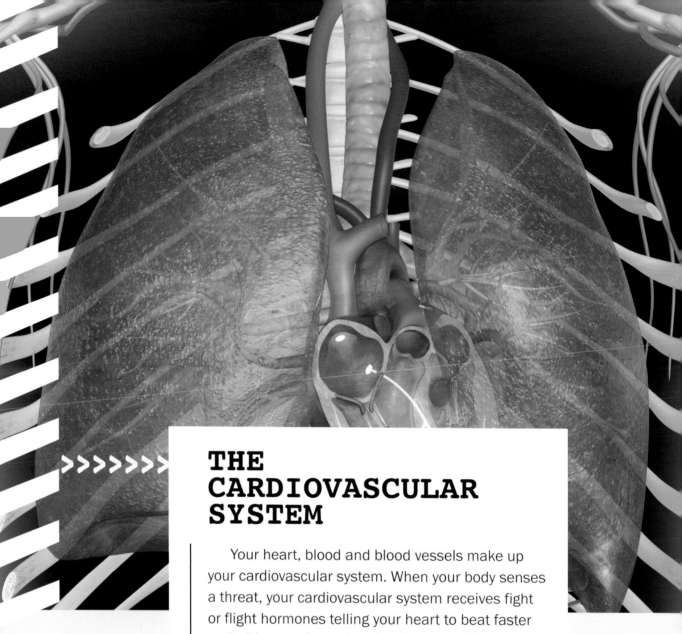

THE CARDIOVASCULAR SYSTEM

>>>>>>>

Your heart, blood and blood vessels make up your cardiovascular system. When your body senses a threat, your cardiovascular system receives fight or flight hormones telling your heart to beat faster and with more force. Arteries that carry blood to the lungs and large muscles widen to increase blood flow. For a fight or flight response, your large muscles require extra oxygen.

At the same time, the cardiovascular system narrows other arteries to reduce the blood flow to parts of the body not needed for fight or flight. These include the stomach, digestive tract, extremities, skin and brain. You may be surprised that your brain gets less blood flow. But in your immediate "danger", you do not need to think. You only need to act. You may feel a bit dizzy or have trouble concentrating.

THE RESPIRATORY SYSTEM

Your lungs, airways and other muscles, such as your diaphragm, make up your respiratory system. This system supplies your body with oxygen and removes carbon dioxide, a waste gas. When your respiratory system is working normally, your diaphragm relaxes and contracts to move air into and out of your lungs. But when something happens that triggers your anxiety, everything changes.

Your brain sends messages to stop breathing with your diaphragm and start breathing with your upper chest muscles. This makes you breathe very fast so extra oxygen can get into your bloodstream. But it also means you breathe out too much carbon dioxide. Without enough carbon dioxide, you might feel light-headed, confused, tingly and numb.

LIFE TIP

When you're feeling anxious or afraid, try to find a quiet room. Take some deep breaths. Think of another time you were nervous. Did things really turn out so bad? Remind yourself of a time everything ended up okay. This might help you feel better.

>>> THE MUSCULAR SYSTEM

You have muscles all over your body that give you the strength to move. Some muscles are voluntary – you control their movements with your thoughts. Your skeletal muscles are voluntary. They are attached to your bones and make your body move. Your smooth muscles are involuntary. Your brain tells them to move without you thinking about it. Smooth muscles are found around organs, such as the stomach and lungs, and inside the walls of the intestines and arteries.

When your fight or flight responses start to kick in, your body tells some of your smooth muscles to contract, such as those under the skin. Your body tells others to relax, such as the diaphragm. Your skeletal muscles get all the attention. Hormones are energising the muscles of your arms, legs and shoulders. But when you do not use that energy, your muscles tighten and your body stays poised to act. You feel tense and jittery.

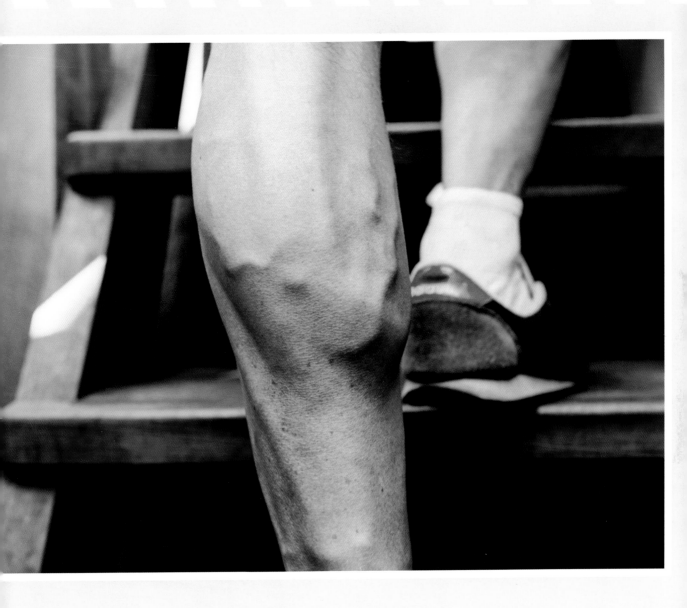

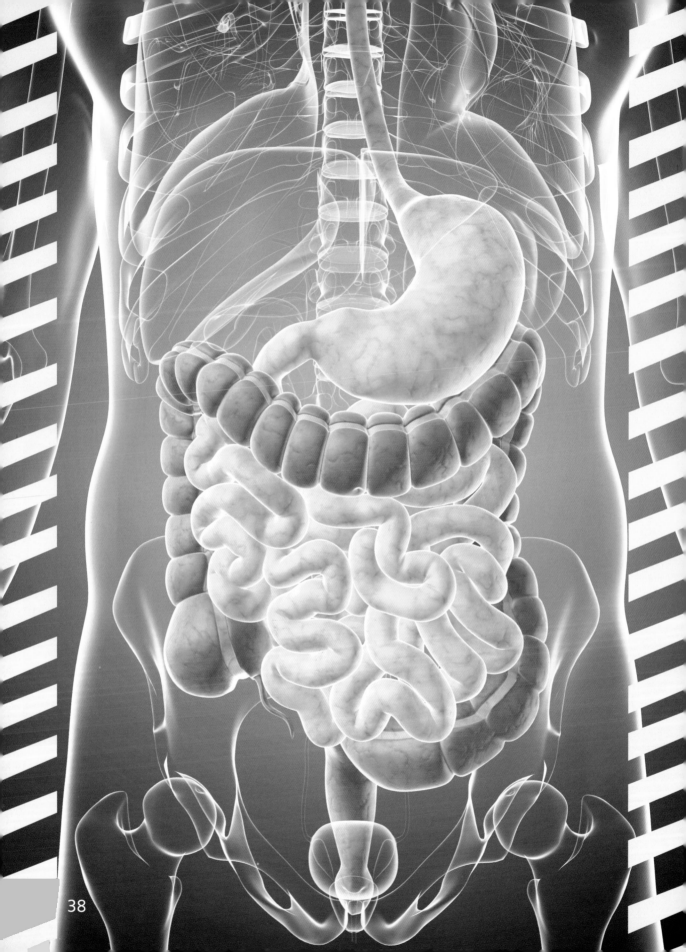

>>>> DIGESTIVE AND EXCRETORY SYSTEMS

The digestive system is what processes the food that you eat. It reacts in two main ways when you feel threatened. First, hormones force your stomach to release extra acid to get rid of any food that might be there. Your breakfast will be digested quickly and turned into extra energy. But once your breakfast is gone, hormones put your digestive system on hold. It is not needed for fight or flight.

The excretory system is what gets rid of waste. It is not needed for fight or flight. When you start feeling threatened, your fight or flight responses are set off. Your muscles tighten around your intestines, and your excretory system slows to a halt. The skin is also part of the excretory system. Hormones make muscles under your skin contract, pushing beads of sweat to the surface. Those tiny muscles are also attached to the hair on your skin. When you feel threatened, those muscles contract and tug on your hair. The tugging makes your hair stand upright and gives you goosebumps.

LIFE TIP

Regular exercise and healthy eating are good choices for everyone. This is especially true for people who are anxious. Some studies have shown that exercise can help calm your body and your mind. Try different exercise routines until you find one that works for you.

CHAPTER 4

WHERE SHYNESS COMES FROM

A lot goes on in your body as it reacts to certain situations. What causes all of this to happen? What makes someone shy? Is it something shy people are born with? Or does shyness come later? It could be both. Scientists are trying to find out.

>>>> GENETICS

You have probably heard people say that you get certain traits from your parents. You may have eyes similar to your dad's or hair similar to your mum's. Is the same true for shyness?

Some scientists studying shyness have observed how babies behave. Some babies were bolder and more excited to play with a new toy or interact with others. Other babies were more timid. They pulled away from new toys and surroundings. They were also more likely to become shy as they got older. This led scientists to believe that children can be born shy and that genes might play a role in how the children behaved.

Scientists are also studying specific genes. The human body has between 20,000 and 30,000 genes. So far scientists have identified a couple that might be responsible for causing shyness.

YOUR ENVIRONMENT

Genetics probably plays a role in shyness. But many experts agree that one's life experiences also play a part. Some children might feel pushed into situations they are not ready for. Over time, this can make them more fearful and shy. Sometimes children who are bullied or teased may become shyer. Other children who have overly cautious parents may be shyer than those who have outgoing parents. People can become shy when their families face challenges or big changes, such as financial problems, divorce or new step-parents and siblings.

Try not to worry too much about whether your shyness comes from your genes or your environment. Focus more on your social goals. Work on those goals. Remember that you don't have to change who you are. It's okay to be a quiet person.

>>> Missy Elliott

Missy Elliott is one of the most successful female hip-hop artists of all time. Yet that doesn't change her fear of performing in front of others. She even required medical attention before performing during a show in 2015. She said in an interview, "I got shyer as I got older and realized people could be laughing at me, or judging me." As a child, Elliott began focusing on music to cope. Focusing on her music has helped her to deal with her fear of performing.

Some people outgrow shyness as they get older and become more comfortable in social situations. Other people may struggle to be more sociable, but there are ways to overcome it for everyone. You just need to find what works for you. You can start with these small steps.

Know yourself. You may sometimes feel like everyone expects you to be louder and more talkative. While it's important to speak up for yourself at the right times, you only need to be as sociable as you wish to be. If you're comfortable being a quiet or more introverted person, that's okay. If you want to be more sociable, then that's a goal you can work towards.

Gain confidence. What do you like about yourself? What do others say are your positive qualities? Focus on these and don't be too hard on yourself when you feel like you've made a mistake.

Get involved. Find clubs, lessons, volunteer opportunities or other activities that speak to you. You'll meet other people who have interests similar to yours. These settings are a great place to practise your social skills and make new friends.

Practise. Start small. Challenge yourself a little bit each day. Find one person you've never talked to before and say hi. Prepare yourself for the next time you meet new people by planning ahead of time what you want to say.

ASK FOR HELP

If you believe you're suffering from anxiety, depression or another mental health issue or are the victim of bullying, ask for help. Reach out to a teacher, parent or another trusted adult. Doctors, psychologists and social workers are available to get you the help you need. You can also reach out to one of these organizations below.

Anti-Bullying Alliance
Offering helplines and advice if you are being bullied.
https://www.anti-bullyingalliance.org.uk

Childline
Online or on-the-phone help, whatever your problem.
https://www.childline.org.uk

Samaritans
You can call or email the Samaritans to talk to someone any time of the day or night.
https://www.samaritans.org

Stem4
Helping teens manage anxiety and mental health issues.
https://stem4.org.uk

Young Minds
Leading the fight for a future where all young minds are supported and empowered, whatever the challenges.
https://www.youngminds.org.uk

FIND OUT MORE

My Anxiety Handbook: Getting Back on Track, Sue Knowles, Bridie Gallagher and Phoebe McEwen (Jessica Kingsley Publishers, 2018)

Relationships (Teen Issues), Lori Hile (Raintree, 2013)

Relationships Whiz: Facts and Figures About Families, Friends and Feelings (Girlology), Elizabeth Raum (Raintree, 2019)

The Anxiety Survival Guide for Teens (Instant Help Solutions), Jennifer Shannon (New Harbinger, 2015)

The Shyness and Social Anxiety Workbook for Teens, Jennifer Shannon (New Harbinger, 2012)

INDEX